C. E Baynes

Album of Indian Ferns

Reproduced in Chromo-Lithography from Original Water-Colour Drawings

C. E Baynes

Album of Indian Ferns
Reproduced in Chromo-Lithography from Original Water-Colour Drawings

ISBN/EAN: 9783337230005

Printed in Europe, USA, Canada, Australia, Japan

Cover: Foto ©Thomas Meinert / pixelio.de

More available books at **www.hansebooks.com**

ALBUM

of

INDIAN FERNS

Reproduced in Chromo-Lithography

FROM ORIGINAL WATER-COLOUR DRAWINGS

BY

C. E. BAYNES.

LONDON:
PUBLISHED BY WILLIAM DAY, 21A, BERNERS STREET.
1887

PREFACE.

ENCOURAGED by the kind wishes of friends, as well as the opinions of less partial advisers, I have ventured to publish my Album of Indian Ferns. In doing so I have simply given them their names, believing that any attempt at fuller description would not add to their value in the eyes of those merely seeking some idea of their natural beauty on their native hills; while it would be unneeded by those already specially interested in the Fern Family, and who will regard them only as renewing or augmenting their acquaintance with it. I would gladly think that some who may glance at the results of my careful study, whether botanists or not, may experience some of the pleasure I enjoyed while pursuing it in my mountain abode on the Shevaroys.

C. E. BAYNES.

LIST OF ILLUSTRATIONS.

PLATE I

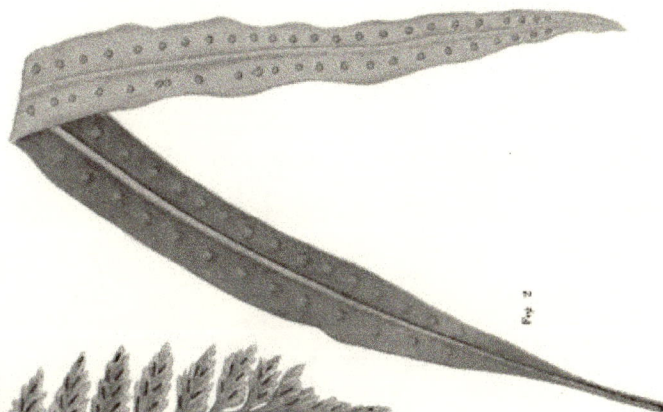

Fig. 2

Fig. 1

PLATE 5

Fig. 3 - Blechnum orientale.

Fig. 3

Fig. 4

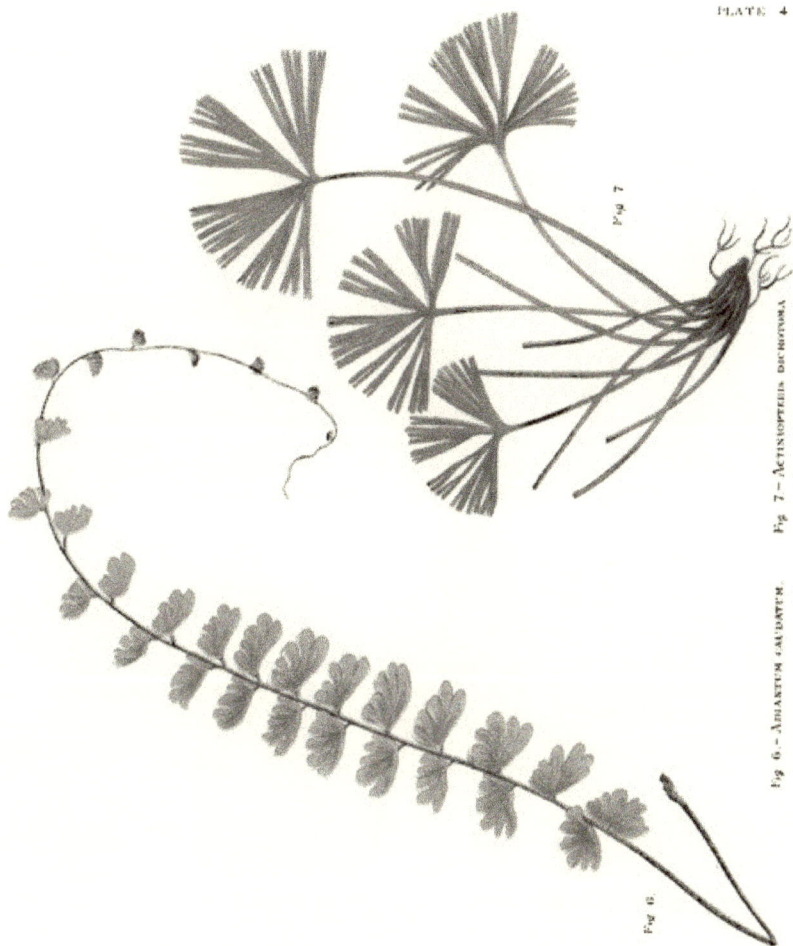

PLATE 4

Fig 7

Fig 6

Fig 6 – ADIANTUM CAUDATUM   Fig 7 – ACTINOPTERIS DICHOTOMA

PLATE 5

Fig. 12.

Fig. 2.

Fig. 11

Fig. 12

Fig. 13

Fig. 14

PLATE 8

Fig. 18.

Fig. 17.

Fig. 16.

Fig. 15.

Fig. 15.—DICKSIA DIVES   Fig. 16.—CHEILANTHES VARIANS   Fig. 17.—CYRTOMIUM CARYOTIDEUM   Fig. 18.—PTERIS GERANIIFOLIA

PLATE 9

Fig. 20.

Fig. 19.

Fig. 19.—CYATHEA SPINULOSA   Fig. 20.—ATHYRIUM FIMBRIATUM

PLATE 10

Fig. 21 – ADIANTUM HISPIDULUM

PLATE 12

Fig. 27.

Fig. 28.

Fig. 29.

Fig. 30.

Fig. 27.— HEMIONITIS CORDATA   Fig. 28.— NEPHROLEPIS CORDIFOLIA   Fig. 30.— NEPHRODIUM MOLLE

PLATE 15

Fig. 30.— Osmunda regalis.

Fig 33

Fig 32

Fig. 33 – POLYPODIUM QUERCIFOLIUM.

www.ingramcontent.com/pod-product-compliance
Lightning Source LLC
Chambersburg PA
CBHW021438090426
42739CB00009B/1544